ART
and
ARTISTS

BUDDHAPADIPA

London UK

Dr Kesorn Pechrach Weaver

ART
and
ARTISTS

BUDDHAPADIPA
London UK

Dr Kesorn Pechrach Weaver

Pechrach Publishing

Art and Artists Buddhapadipa London UK
By Dr Kesorn Pechrach Weaver

ISBN 978-1-912957-02-6

PECHRACH PUBLISHING
7 Boundary Road, Bishops Stortford, Hertfordshire, CM23 5LE, England, United Kingdom. Tel: (+44) 1279 508020, +44 (0) 7443426937

Published 2019 by Pechrach Publishing
Copyright © 2019 Kesorn Pechrach Weaver and Pechrach Publishing

The right of Kesorn Pechach Weaver to be identified as the author of this work has been asserted in accordance with section 77 and 78 of the Copyright, Designs and Patents Act 1988

All right reserved. No part of this publication may be reproduced, stored in a retrieval system, or transmitted in any form or by any means, electronic, mechanical, photocopying, recording, or otherwise, without the prior permission of the publishers.

Every reasonable attempt has been made to identify owners of copyright. Errors or omissions will be corrected in subsequent editions. Although the authors and publisher have made every effort to ensure that the information in this book was correct at the time of going to press, the authors and publisher do not assume and hereby disclaim any liability to any party for any loss, damage, or disruption caused by errors or omissions.

This book is dedicated to

Thai Artists

Acknowledgments

I would like to thank and pay my respect to my son, Master Neran James Pechrach Weaver for giving me inspiration to write this book when he become a novice monk during summer school holiday August 2018.

I also would like to thank Artist Kitisak Nuelluck and Artist Areeporn Nuelluck for telling me their story.

I would like to thank Dr Paul M Weaver for all support while preparing materials for this book.

Thanks to any volunteer, who help do many jobs includes cooking, gardening, services and anything in the Buddhapadipa Temple.

Many Thanks to my family in Thailand includes Somjan Pechrach, Amporn Pechrach, Pramoun Krainoonka, Somchai Krainoonka, Somruithai Krainoonka, Ekkavit Krainoonka and Kunsin Rattanavaru, for always believe in me.

Finally, I would like to thank: Rung Ratpinyotip Scott and Dr. Sirilaksana Kunjara for their support to write this book.

Message from Author

The author always wants to write this book while spending time in the Buddahapadipa temple for many days when my son becomes the novice monk.

The pictures in the Ubosatha hall at the Buddhapadipa temple are so beautiful. However, there are many pictures are not matched at the same period, some are ancient and some are modern.

Moreover, some pictures are more than I can imaginary. However, it is not easy to understand the meaning behind those pictures. Nevertheless, most of the pictures are about the life of the Buddha and his Dhamma.

Fortunately, I meet the couple, who are the original artists. They are the team drawing and painting the pictures in the Ubosatha hall since 1987. Nowadays, some of those pictures are old and need some repairing and they are the person who does the jobs.

I hope this book would be useful as a basic and rough guide to learn and have a better understanding about the picture in the Ubosatha hall, Buddhapadipa temple, London, UK.

Dr. Kesorn P. Weaver

7th January 2019

United Kingdom

Table of Contents

Acknowledgement

Message from Author

Chapter 1: Buddhapadipa Temple	1
Chapter 2: Meet the Artists	9
Chapter 3: Artist Kitisak's Work and Life	19
Chapter 4: Teams of Artists	28
Chapter 5: Pictures Concept	41
Chapter 6: Pictures Tone	48
Chapter 7: Pictures Plan 1-4	61
Chapter 8: Pictures Plan 5-7	73
Chapter 9: Pictures Plan 8-10	87
Chapter 10: Pictures Plan 11	101
Chapter 11: Pictures Plan 12	111
Chapter 12: Pictures Plan 13-14	121
Chapter 13: Pictures Plan 15-16	130
Chapter 14: Pictures Plan 17	136
References	146

Table of Figures

CHAPTER 1: Buddhapadipa Temple   1

Figure 1.1: Novice monk ceremony   1

Figure 1.2: Wat Buddhapadipa   2

Figure 1.3: Front gate Wat Buddhapadipa   3

Figure 1.4: The Novice monks at the main building   4

Figure 1.5: Wat Buddhapadipa fence   4

Figure 1.6: The Uposatha Hall   5

Figure 1.7: Fence around the Uposatha Hall   6

Figure 1.8: Thai Architecture   6

Figure 1.9: Four entrance to Uposatha hall   7

Figure 1.10: Bell tower building next to the lake   7

Figure 1.11: Teacing Thamma outdoor   8

CHAPTER 2: Meet the Artists   9

Figure 2.1: Kitisak and Areeporn as volunteers at the Buddhapapida Temple   9

Figure 2.2: Volunteers serving food to the novice monks   10

Figure 2.3: Volunteers work in the kitchen   11

Figure 2.4: Volunteers take care the novice monks visit the Wimbledon tennis courts   12

Figure 2.5: Volunteers look after the monks when go out   12

Figure 2.6: Volunteers prepare hot drinks	13
Figure 2.7: Artist Kitisak Nuelluck in his free time	14
Figure 2.8: Artist Kitisak drawing	15
Figure 2.9: Hand sketch lotus picture	16
Figure 2.10: Artist Areeporn Nuelluck prepare food for the monks	16
Figure 2.11: Lists of the artists involve in the Uposatha hall painting	17
Figure 2.12: Artist Kitisak and his proud paintings	17
Figure 2.13: Explain the meaning of the pictures	18
CHAPTER 3: Artist Kitisak's Work and Life	19
Figure 3.1: Volunteers artist at the Buddhapadipa Temple	19
Figure 3.2: Art students	20
Figure 3.3: Art students at Silpakorn University, Thailand	21
Figure 3.4: Art students at Silpakorn University, Thailand	21
Figure 3.5: Artist Kitisak Nuallak's exhibition	22
Figure 3.6: Artist Kitisak Nuallak's exhibition	22
Figure 3.7: Artist Kitisak Nuallak's exhibition	23
Figure 3.8: Artist Kitisak Nuallak's exhibition	24
Figure 3.9: Artist Kitisak Nuallak's exhibition	25
Figure 3.10: Draft King of Mara drawing by artist Kitisak Nuallak	26

Figure 3.11: Draft the lotus drawing by artist Kitisak Nuallak	27

CHAPTER 4: Teams of Artists	28
Figure 4.1: A Group of volunteer artists	28
Figure 4.2: Artist Chalermchai and team work	29
Figure 4.3: Artist Chalwermchai Kositpipat (left) and artist Panya Vijinthanasarn (right)	30
Figure 4.4: Artist Panya works on the site	30
Figure 4.5: Artist Kitisak Nuelluck	31
Figure 4.6: Artist Chalwermchai Kositpipat (left) and artist Panya Vijinthanasarn (right)	32
Figure 4.7: Artist Areeporn and Artist Kitisak	32
Figure 4.8: Volunteer artist Areeporn Suwannanupong	33
Figure 4.9: Artist Areeporn Suwannanupong	34
Figure 4.10: Artist teams, their sponsors, and artist Artist Areeporn Suwannanupong	35
Figure 4.11: Artist Areeporn and Kitisak wedding	36
Figure 4.12: Artist Kitisak repairs the pictures	37
Figure 4.13: Artist Kitisak repairs the picture wall	38
Figure 4.14: Artist Areeporn repairs the pictures	38
Figure 4.15: Artist Kitisak copies the pictures	39
Figure 4.16: Repairing the pictures with their daughter, Pimpun Nuelluck	40

CHAPTER 5: Pictures Concept	41
Figure 5.1: Wall pictures inside the Ubosatha Hall	41
Figure 5.2: The wall and ceiling inside the Ubosatha Hall, Buddhapadipa temple	42
Figure 5.3: The big picture of flighting the King Mara	43
Figure 5.4: The story of the Buddha pictures	43
Figure 5.5: The president Buddha	44
Figure 5.6: The Buddha defeats the Mara	45
Figure 5.7: The birth and Buddha	46
Figure 5.8: The death and Nirvana	47
CHAPTER 6: Pictures Tone	48
Figure 6.1: Dreaming picture colour tone	48
Figure 6.2: War zone colour tone picture	49
Figure 6.3: The trees with detail flowers pictures	49
Figure 6.4: Houses and trees pictures	50
Figure 6.5: Buddha colour tone in war zone	51
Figure 6.6: Proportion the building and the human	51
Figure 6.7: Monk colour tone picture	52
Figure 6.8: Buddha colour tone picture	52
Figure 6.9: Western arts inside the picture	53
Figure 6.10: The nuclear bomb	53
Figure 6.11: Robots War	54
Figure 6.12: The chemical weapon	54
Figure 6.13: Thai Airways and Van Gogh Vincent	55
Figure 6.14: International Army	56

Figure 6.15: British Army   57
Figure 6.16: The USA Rocket   57
Figure 6.17: The King of Mara colour tone picture   58
Figure 6.18: The royal family pictures   59
Figure 6.19: The common people pictures   60

CHAPTER 7: Pictures Plan 1-4   61
Figure 7.1: The Ubosatha hall layout of the mother's dream picture   61
Figure 7.2: The mother's dream (green circle picture)   62
Figure 7.3: The mother's dream   63
Figure 7.4: The Ubosatha hall layout of the birth picture   64
Figure 7.5: The birth pictures (green circle picture)   65
Figure 7.6: The birth pictures   66
Figure 7.7: The Ubosatha hall layout of the five revelations dream picture   67
Figure 7.8: The dream of five revelations (green circle picture)   68
Figure 7.9: The dream of five   69
Figure 7.10: The Ubosatha hall layout of the casting the tray fortune picture   70
Figure 7.11: The casting the tray fortune (green circle picture)   71
Figure 7.12: The casting the tray   72

CHAPTER 8: Pictures Plan 5-7 73
Figure 8.1: The Ubosatha hall layout of the fight with the King of Mara picture 73
Figure 8.2: The fight with the King of Mara (green circle picture) 74
Figure 8.3: The Buddha defeats the King of Mara 75
Figure 8.4: The Earth Goddess (green circle picture) 76
Figure 8.5: The Ubosatha hall layout of the four levels of lotus picture 77
Figure 8.6: The four levels of lotus on the right wall corner (green circle picture) 78
Figure 8.7: The four levels of lotus 79
Figure 8.8: The four levels of lotus 80
Figure 8.9: The four levels of lotus 81
Figure 8.10: The four levels of lotus 82
Figure 8.11: The four levels of lotus on the right wall centre (green circle picture) 83
Figure 8.12: The Ubosatha hall layout of the first sermon picture 84
Figure 8.13: The first sermon (green circle picture) 85
Figure 8.14: The first sermon 86

CHAPTER 9: Pictures Plan 8-10 87
Figure 9.1: The Ubosatha hall layout of the Thammajakra Kappawatana Sutra picture 87
Figure 9.2: The Thammajakra Kappawatana Sutra 88

(green circle picture)

Figure 9.3: The loose discipline	89
Figure 9.4: The extreme self mortification	90
Figure 9.5: The Ubosatha hall layout of the Buddha teaches the Dhamma to his mother and go to teach in the Hell World picture	92
Figure 9.6: Teach Dhamma to mother (green circle picture)	93
Figure 9.7: The Buddha teaches Dhamma to his mother	94
Figure 9.8: The Buddha descent from the heaven to teach the Dhamma to the Hell World	95
Figure 9.9: The Ubosatha hall layout of the two miracles picture	96
Figure 9.10: The two miracles (green circle picture)	97
Figure 9.11: The first miracle	97
Figure 9.12: The Buddha's students perform fly action to get the bowl down	98
Figure 9.13: The second miracle	99
CHAPTER 10: Pictures Plan 11	101
Figure 10.1: The Ubosatha hall layout of the eight miracles picture	101
Figure 10.2: The eight miracles (green circle picture)	102
Figure 10.3: The second miracles defeating the King of Mara Wasawadi	103

Figure 10.4: The second miracles defeating the giant Alawaka	104
Figure 10.5: The third miracles defeating the elephant Nakakiri	105
Figure 10.6: The fourth miracles defeating the thief Angkhuliman	106
Figure 10.7: The fifth miracles defeating the woman Jinjamanavika	107
Figure 10.8: The sixth miracles defeating the heretic Satjakanikkaron	108
Figure 10.9: The seventh miracles defeating the Naga Nantopananta	109
Figure 10.10: The eighth miracles defeating the Thao Pakabrahma	110
CHAPTER 11: Pictures Plan 12	111
Figure 11.1: The Ubosatha hall layout of the Buddha action for every day in a week picture	111
Figure 11.2: The Sunday to Wednesday Buddha (green circle picture)	112
Figure 11.3: Figure 11.3: The Thursday to Saturday Buddha (green circle picture)	113
Figure 11.4: The Sunday Buddha	114
Figure 11.5: The Monday Buddha	115
Figure 11.6: The Tuesday Buddha	116
Figure 11.7: The Wednesday Buddha	117

Figure 11.8: The Thursday Buddha	118
Figure 11.9: The Friday Buddha	119
Figure 11.10: The Saturday Buddha	120
CHAPTER 12: Pictures Plan 13-14	121
Figure 12.1: The Ubosatha hall layout of the celestial assembly picture	121
Figure 12.2: The celestial assembly on the far end of the left wall (green circle picture)	122
Figure 12.3: The celestial assembly on the birth of the Buddha	122
Figure 12.4: The celestial assembly on the corner left wall (green circle picture)	123
Figure 12.5: The celestial assembly on the birth of the Buddha	123
Figure 12.6: The celestial assembly on the right corner (green circle picture)	124
Figure 12.7: The celestial assembly on the death of the Buddha	124
Figure 12.8: The celestial assembly on the far end of the right wall (green circle picture)	125
Figure 12.9: The celestial assembly on the death of the Buddha	125
Figure 12.10: The Ubosatha hall layout of the Mara King asks the Buddha to death and the Buddha's last meal pictures	126

Figure 12.11: Mara King asks the Buddha to death or Nirvana (green circle picture)	127
Figure 12.12: The King of Mara and the Buddha	127
Figure 12.13: The last meal (green circle picture)	128
Figure 12.14: The Buddha's last meal	129
Figure 12.15: The Buddha becomes ill	129
CHAPTER 13: Pictures Plan 15-16	130
Figure 13.1: The Ubosatha hall layout of the death of the Buddha picture	130
Figure 13.2: The death of the Buddha or the Nirvana (green circle picture)	131
Figure 13.3: The death of the Buddha	131
Figure 13.4: The Ubosatha hall layout of the flower Montha and the Buddha's relics picture	133
Figure 13.5: The divided the Buddha's relics (green circle picture)	134
Figure 13.6: The Montha flower	135
Figure 13.7: The divided the Buddha's relics	135
CHAPTER 14: Pictures Plan 17	136
Figure 14.1: The Ubosatha hall layout of the three world pictures	136
Figure 14.2: The three worlds (green circle picture)	137
Figure 14.3: The Hell world	137
Figure 14.4: The Hell World (green circle picture)	138

Figure 14.5: The Buddha in the Hell World 138

Figure 14.6: The Human World (green circle picture) 139

Figure 14.7: The people in the Human World 140

Figure 14.8: The monks in the Human World 141

Figure 14.9: The Buddha reaches the enlightenment in the Human World 142

Figure 14.10: The Heaven World (green circle picture) 143

Figure 14.11: The six Heaven above the Sithandara Ocean 143

Figure 14.12: The three heavens on the right and three on the left 144

Figure 14.13: The sixteen Brahma levels 144

Figure 14.14: The four non- form Prahma 145

Figure 14.15: The list of Buddha 145

CHAPTER 1
Buddhapadipa Temple

Figure 1.1: Novice monk ceremony

I have lived in the United Kindom nearly 20 years. However, this is my second time visiting the Buddhapadipa Temple. It is because the distance from my house is pretty far and also it is in London. As we know, everything in London, the capital of the United Kingdom is very expensive, especially the transportation and time consuming.

The main reason for me to visit the Buddhapadipa temple again after my first visiting in 2008. At that time my son just over 6 months old. We brought him here for his first hair cutting ceremony. In the year 2018, he is just over 11 years old and I would like him to earn experience as a novice monk. That is the main reason for us to visit the Buddhapadipa temple again.

As a mother and a Buddhist, my experience of practise meditation. I have known that the meditation would help my son to deal with the changing situation and cope with the changing. Not only in his secondary school, but be a teenage in the near future for him.

Therefore, we try to find out where and how he can learn basic and a place where he practice of meditating. In the safe environment, the teacher can teach the meditation methodology in English and the important thing is the place must not be very far from us to make a visit from time to time. The learning and Practise place must be in the United Kingdom, where most people can speak English very well. He will familiar with the weather as well as the environment.

Figure 1.2: Wat Buddhapadipa

Figure 1.3: Front gate Wat Buddhapadipa

There are information about the summer Samanera training course at the webpage http://www.padipa.org/ and http://www.watbuddhapadipa.org

The Buddhapadipa Temple, Wimbledon, London, has a program for ordination of Novices Monks or as known as the Summer Samanera Training Course, which they held the event every year during the summer holiday. It is a good opportunity for boys to learn about the Buddhist and the way that the monks live, including learning meditation at the same time.

We make a telephone call at the number +44 (0) 208 946 1357 to find out more information about the Summer Samanera and make an appointment for visiting the temple. We know it is not easy for us to drive direct pass the centre of London, United Kingdom. There are many congestion zones and low carbon emission zones to pay for the charge.

Figure 1.4: The Novice monks at the main building

Figure 1.5: Wat Buddhapadipa fence

When our car drives pass the temple gate. We can feel just like we are in a different world, quiet, peaceful and happy.

The Uposatha hall building is very beautiful and there is the same plan as the Buddhists Wat in Thailand. The layout and the set up is the standard with a white concrete fence around the building. There are four stair entrances to the upper level, which fence up around the top of the Uposatha Hall.

Figure 1.6: The Uposatha Hall

The building with Wat Thai architecture standing in the middle of the big grass area next to the lake with there are various birds and ducks.

I have read some books about the Uposatha Hall in the Buddhapadipa temple before. The architecture, construction and artists were all Thais and they came from Thailand to build this building.

The main construction of the building was finished in a few years. However, The painting inside the building and the decoration, which need to be done by the Thai artists only. Those tasks took a long time and many years before it is completed.

Figure 1.7: Fence around the Uposatha Hall

Figure 1.8: Thai Architecture

It just likes we have got lost in the different world, not in the London, which is the capital of the United Kingdom. The most busy working lifestyle and the world capital of financing, which we just passed by less than a few minutes ago..

Figure 1.9: Four entrance to Uposatha hall

Figure 1.10: Bell tower building next to the lake

The big plot of land and garden, there are a pond and forest in the same area. It is like a real museum and the temple in the same place The Bell tower building was painted with red colour standing beside the lake next to the main building, which used as head office and a place where all of the monks stay.

The green grass garden around the Ubosatha hall is used for outdoor learning Thamma and walking meditation. There are many kinds of trees and some of them are older than the Buddhapadipa temple. The area used to be the forest with the natural lake. Thus, there are many wild animals and beautiful rare birds visit the garden so often.

Figure 1.11: Teacing Thamma outdoor

CHAPTER 2
Meet the Artists

Figure 2.1: Kitisak and Areeporn as volunteers at the Buddhapapida Temple

During half a month that my son became the novice monk, I also learn a lot of life of the monks and people, who work as volunteers in the Buddhapadipa temple. The place is very big to maintain by the monks. This is not only the buildings, but also the ground area.

Figure 2.2: Volunteers serving food to the novice monks

A number of volunteers have come to help every day, start from early morning in the kitchen until evening when they offer the evening meditation course for general interest.

The first time I met the artist Kitisak. He is one of the main volunteers, who responsible to look after the group of novice monks and my son was in this group. This task is for the male volunteer only since women are not allowed to make a physical contact with the monk. Therefore, it is the man's job.

While his wife, artist Areeporn loves to work in the kitchen. Her duty would include cleaning, washing up and prepare food for the monks.

Figure 2.3: Volunteers work in the kitchen

Both of them work as the artist and volunteer in the Buddhapadipa temple for many years before they do various jobs not only in the main building, but also the garden. It would count more than 30 years since they have been living in the United Kingdom.

Another reason why it needs to be a man. His may lay on they are the same sex to the monks. Also, man talk and discussion are different from woman. That may be easy to communicate and get the job done quickly.

Figure 2.4: Volunteers take care the novice monks visit the Wimbledon tennis courts

Figure 2.5: Volunteers look after the monks when go out

Figure 2.6: Volunteers prepare hot drinks

As we known the monks cannot serve themselves food or drinks. Therefore, the caretaker would offer them when they go out. One of the duty of the artist Kitisak is to look after the monks and be the monk's caretaker when they go out.

His jobs would start very early in the morning before everybody else gets up. His duty, includes preparing breakfast and hot drinks for the monks and novice monks.

His alarm clock would wake him up at 4 AM to help in the kitchen and prepare breakfast both Thai style for the monks and English breakfast for the novice monks. This is because most of the novice monks were born in the United Kingdom and they are familiar with the British food more than Thai food. The breakfast has to be ready to serve between 5 AM-7 AM.

Figure 2.7: Artist Kitisak Nuelluck in his free time

During his free time between breakfast and lunch, he likes to practise his drawing, which is inside his mind and his hands process in the drawing sketching. He shows me a quick drawing the picture of lotus after a few minutes later. He looks very happy while he does any activities with drawing and paintings. He has a lot of pictures and his paints collections

Figure 2.8: Artist Kitisak drawing

30 years ago, he was offered a job to paint the pictures inside the Ubosatha hall at the Buddhapadipa, Wimbledon, London, UK. Since then until now, his life and his family have involved in the Buddhapadipa temple.

In front of the Uposatha hall, next to the main building, there is a monument with a list of artists' name. He shows me where is his name in the list when he worked as the artist paints the picture inside the Ubosatha hall.

He told me his story and how he becomes a volunteer in the Buddhapadipa temple. He said he came to the United Kingdom more than 30 years ago, when he just finished his first degree in arts from Silapakorn University, Bangkok, Thailand.

Figure 2.9: Hand sketch lotus picture

Figure 2.10: Artist Areeporn Nuelluck prepare food for the monks

Figure 2.11: Lists of the artists involve in the Uposatha hall painting

Figure 2.12: Artist Kitisak and his proud paintings

Figure 2.13: Explain the meaning of the pictures

He explains the meaning behind each of the pictures inside the Ubosatha hall. There are many pictures could not find any meaning. However, in the eyes of the artists, eery pictures have their own information.

CHAPTER 3
Artist Kitisak's Work and Life

Figure 3.1: Volunteers artist at the Buddhapadipa Temple

Artist Kitisak told me his story, it was more than 30 years ago, around 1984-1987 when he first arrived in the United Kingdom as one of the volunteer artists to design and paints in the pictures in the Ubosatha hall at the Buddhapadipa temple, Wimbledon, London, UK.

The mural paintings are famous in the most of the Buddhist Wat in Thailand. Most of the pictures would be the story of the Budda since he was born, grown up, married, become the Budda, teaching Thamma and pass away.

Artist Kitisak Nuelluck is the graphic designers of the murals painting the last ten Buddha's lives. In addition, he is in the team of the murals painting the Nirvana and the Traiphum with the lead artist Chalerchai Kositpipat.

Artist Kitisak Nuallak was born on 28 June 1963 in Bangkok, Thailand. He graduated Bachelor degree in Thai Arts, Faculty of Sculpture and graphic arts, Silpakorn University, Thailand.

Figure 3.2: Art students

Figure 3.3: Art students at Silpakorn University, Thailand

Figure 3.4: Art students at Silpakorn University, Thailand

Figure 3.5: Artist Kitisak Nuallak's exhibition

Figure 3.6: Artist Kitisak Nuallak's exhibition

Figure 3.7: Artist Kitisak Nuallak's exhibition

Artist Kitisak has a number of exhibitions when he was a student at the Silpakorn University, Thailand during 1981-1995.

This includes art education, vocational arts, art thesis exhibition, mural project at the Buddhapadipa temple, Thai art exhibition in Bangkok, Thailand.

In addition, he received many awards such as the second prize in line drawing and honour prize at the vocational art school, the third prize and the honourable prize for the ceramic competition awards. Furthermore, he receives a scholarship from the Bangkok Bank and a special grant of the Phraya Narisaranuwatiwong.

Figure 3.8: Artist Kitisak Nuallak's exhibition

Figure 3.9: Artist Kitisak Nuallak's exhibition

Figure 3.10: Draft King of Mara drawing by artist Kitisak Nuallak

Figure 3.11: Draft the lotus drawing by artist Kitisak Nuallak

CHAPTER 4
Teams of Artists

Figure 4.1: A Group of volunteer artists

There are three working artist teams worked on the wall painting in the Ubosatha hall at the Buddhapadipa temple.

The first team is the Nirvana and the three worlds. The team members are as follows:

1. Chalermchai Kositpipat

2. Suwan Komtiprat
3. Daeng Kutpet
4. Kitisak Nuelluck
5. Prasat Chandarasupa
6. Rerngsak Boontavanishkul
7. Niramol Rerngsom
8. Surapol Jinarat
9. Thongchai Srisukprasert
10. Teravat Kanama
11. Alongkorn Lauwatana
12. Kanokwan Nakaapi
13. Areeporn Suwannanupong

Figure 4.2: Artist Chalermchai and team work

Figure 4.3: Artist Chalwermchai Kositpipat (left) and artist Panya Vijinthanasarn (right)

Figure 4.4: Artist Panya works on the site

Figure 4.5: Artist Kitisak Nuelluck

The second team is the Birth and the Enlightenment. The team members are as follows:

1. Panya Vijinthanasarn
2. Sompop Budrat
3. Pichit Tungcharoen
4. Sak Khunpolpitak
5. Pusit Ooodasongkram
6. Boonkwang Noncharoen
7. Sanan Sinchalam
8. Prakit Kobkitwatana
9. Nopadol Ithipongsakul
10. Pisal Poavises
11. Apichai Piromrak
12. Sithichoke Konnak

Figure 4.6: Artist Chalwermchai Kositpipat (left) and artist Panya Vijinthanasarn (right)

Figure 4.7: Artist Areeporn and Artist Kitisak

The third team is the Last ten lives. The team members are as follows:

1. Pang Chinasai
2. Sompop Budrat

3. Kitisak Nuelluck
4. Sanan Sinchalam
5. Sak Khunpolpitak
6. Niramol Rerngsom
7. Boonkwang Noncharoen
8. Pusit Poodsongkram
9. Suwan Komtiprat
10. Prida Suetrong
11. Pichai Lertsuwansri
12. Areeporn Suwannanupong
13. Sukanya Budrat

Figure 4.8: Volunteer artist Areeporn Suwannanupong

One of the volunteer artists who join the team to paints the Ubosatha hall at the Buddhapadipa temple, is artist Areeporn.

Figure 4.9: Artist Areeporn Suwannanupong

Artist Areeporn worked on the team of the Nirvana and the three worlds, under the Artist leader Chalermchai Kositpipat, who is the graphic designer of the murals depicting of the Nirvana and the three worlds.

Moreover, she also worked on the project the Last ten lives, which artist Sompop Budrat, artist Pang Chinasai and artist Kitisak Nuelluck are the main graphic designers of the murals depicting.

Figure 4.10: Artist teams, their sponsors, and artist Artist Areeporn Suwannanupong

Figure 4.11: Artist Areeporn and Kitisak wedding

Artist Kitisak and Artist Areeporn had worked together on the Buddhapadipa project for many years and they got married in 1989.

Since then until now, they have lived in London, United Kingdom. Their lives involve not only as the artists, but also as volunteers to look after the monks, maintain the building, gardens, areas and cooking in the kitchen.

Artist Kitisak and Artist Areeporn have looked after the painting for more than 30 years ago. Although the design, drawing and painting all completed since 1989, however, with the hazardous weather in the United Kingdom. There are some pictures have cranked and damaged. Therefore, they need to be repaired. Of course, the person who can do this job, it has to be the person who understands the pictures and paints.

Figure 4.12: Artist Kitisak repairs the pictures

Figure 4.13: Artist Kitisak repairs the picture wall

Figure 4.14: Artist Areeporn repairs the pictures

Figure 4.15: Artist Kitisak copies the pictures

Figure 4.16: Repairing the pictures with their daughter, Pimpun Nuelluck

CHAPTER 5
Pictures Concept

Figure 5.1: Wall pictures inside the Ubosatha Hall

Artist Kitiak told me about the concept and criteria of the pictures and painting in the Ubosatha hall at the Buddhapadipa temple. He said most of the volunteer artists have gone back to Thailand after the job finished. However, he has continued living in London since then until now.

The main concept of the pictures inside the Ubosatha hall is mixed between European art and Thailand culture together with Budda's story. The mural painting in the Buddhapadipa temple is different from the original Uposatha hall in Thailand not only the technique, but also the layout of the pictures.

Figure 5.2: The wall and ceiling inside the Ubosatha Hall, Buddhapadipa temple

The ceiling inside the Ubosatha hall is bright red colour and full of details. The pictures are painted on the whole wall until it reaches the ceiling. There is no gap or empty space.

Most of the mural pictures in Wat Thai in Thailand always put the sequence of pictures as a story. However, the order of the pictures in the Buddhapadipa temple would count the main picture as the most important. Therefore, it has the biggest size. The second important picture has the smaller size.

Figure 5.3: The big picture of flighting the King Mara

The picture of the Buddha flights the army of the King of Mara is on the entrance door. The size of the picture is big. This shows that the story is important. This is because this flighting leads to the enlightenment.

Figure 5.4: The story of the Buddha pictures

In addition, the colour of the pictures in the Buddhapadipa temple is bright colour. They use acrylic paints instead as the chalk as original in Wat Thai in Thailand.

Most of the pictures in the Ubosatha hall are deep in details, not only in the walls, but also the pictures on the ceiling. All of the pictures are painted in the three dimensions and it has the same proportion of the animals and human pictures.

The picture layout in the Ubosatha Hall at the Buddhapadipa Temple, Wimbledon, United Kingdom, have divided into 4 walls. This system is widely used in most of the Wat Thai in Thailand.

5.1 The First Wall

Figure 5.5: The president Buddha

The first wall is the wall behind the president Buddha. The pictures on this wall would be about Three worlds and the Buddha in the heaven. The three worlds are including the Hell World, the Human World and the Heaven World.

However, in this wall is emphasized in the Heaven World in details, but shows some boundary between the human world and the heaven world clearly.

5.2 The Second Wall

Figure 5.6: The Buddha defeats the Mara

The second wall is the wall opposite, which is the main entrance. The pictures on this wall would be about enlightenment and defeat the Mara.

5.3 The Third Wall

Figure 5.7: The birth and Buddha

The third wall is on the left hand side of the presiding Buddha. The pictures on this wall would be about the Birth of the Buddha. This would start from the mother's dream before getting pregnant. Then, the birth in the forest between she visited her parents home. It is a culture that the woman has to travel back to her parents' house for giving birth of her children. However, in this case the baby was born earlier than they expected.

5.4 The Fourth Wall

Figure 5.8: The death and Nirvana

The fourth wall is on the right hand of the president Buddha. The pictures on this wall would be about the death of the Buddha and Nirvana. The pictures would be about the King of Mara asked the Buddha to die, the Buddha has his last meal and the death of the Buddha.

CHAPTER 6

Pictures Tone

There are three main paint colours, which used in the pictures in the Ubosatha hall at the Buddhapadipa temple. They are blue, red and gold. The ratio between red and blue are equal. The colour tone of each picture would be different depending upon the meaning behind the story.

Figure 6.1: Dreaming picture colour tone

The picture about dreaming, the artists would use the blur and not clear sharp line colour. This is because it is the dream, not the real event.

While the bright, red, blue, purple colours with extreme contrast, would use for fighting or war zone. However, the colour tone for the Buddha would be happy, calm, bright cold colour. Opposite to the angry, upset, unhappy colours would use it for the King of Mara and the evil army.

Figure 6.2: War zone colour tone picture

Figure 6.3: The trees with detail flowers pictures

Figure 6.4: Houses and trees pictures

Most of the natural pictures such as mountains, river, trees and forests, the artists would draw and give them colours in real and close to the natural world and drawing the figures in details.

They would use the lighter green and dark green colours of the trees and forests, the brown colour of the houses as made of woods as the materials. However, some pictures show in the idealistic, more than the realistic world. However, some plant colours reflect the four European seasons: spring, summer, autumn, and winter.

Figure 6.5: Buddha colour tone in war zone

For the buildings, landscape and architectures, most of the pictures were shown in Thai culture style. However, there are some pictures of the British architecture in three dimensions.

Figure 6.6: Proportion the building and the human

Figure 6.7: Monk colour tone picture

Figure 6.8: Buddha colour tone picture

In addition, the proportion between the building and the human may not be real. The human may look bigger than the building. This is because the artists would like to show the human activities, which is the main character of these pictures.

However, there are some parts in these pictures would insert the real western arts in some pictures. There are some pictures of the famous people insert in those pictures.

Figure 6.9: Western arts inside the picture

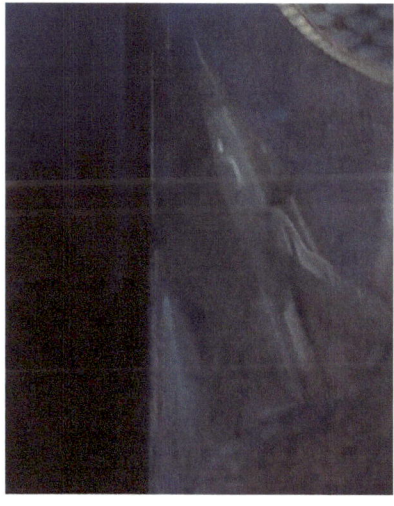

Figure 6.10: The nuclear bomb

Figure 6.11: Robots War

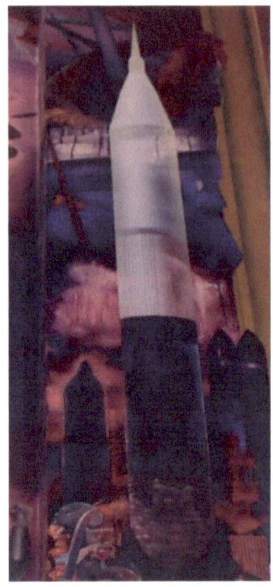

Figure 6.12: The chemical weapon

Figure 6.13: Thai Airways and Van Gogh Vincent

One of them is the air plane from the Thai airways. This is because they one of the sponsors for paints.

Figure 6.14: International Army

Figure 6.15: British Army

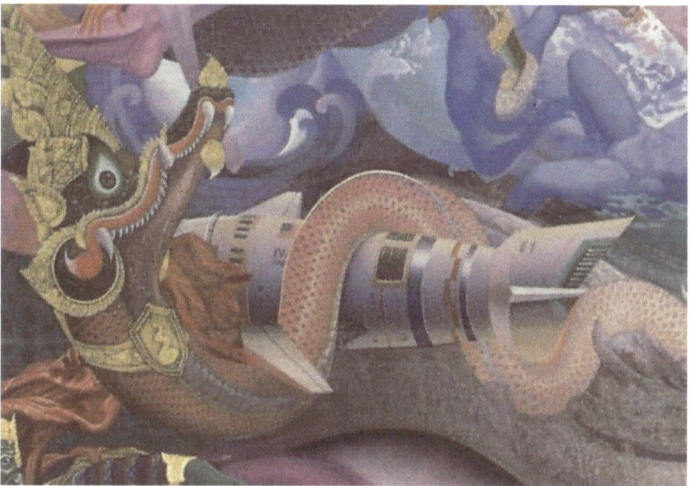

Figure 6.16: The USA Rocket

There are completely mixed between the real world and the imaginary world in most of the pictures.

Figure 6.17: The King of Mara colour tone picture

There are two groups of human in the paints in the Ubosatha, Buddhapadipa temple. The first group is the King, Queen, Prince, Princess and the Royal family. The artists would draw and paint them to look smart. They would have their hands act to show their emotions.

Figure 6.18: The royal family pictures

The second group is the common people. The artists would draw them to have fun and enjoy emotion. In addition, some human pictures are the real people who are present in the real world.

Figure 6.19: The common people pictures

The most important of the pictures in the Ubosatha hall at the Buddhapadipa temple is the art and the emotion of each picture. However, the story of the Buddha is also the main story from birth, enlightenment, the first sermon and the nirvana. This includes some pictures of the celestial and three worlds.

CHAPTER 7
Pictures Plan 1-4

The Picture 1: The mother's dream

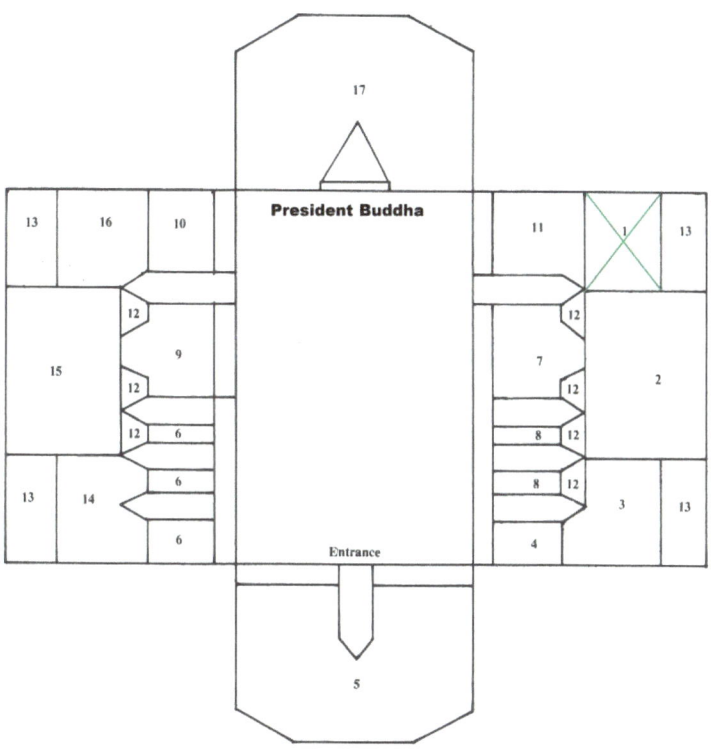

Figure 7.1: The Ubosatha hall layout of the mother's dream picture

Figure 7.2: The mother's dream (green circle picture)

This picture is about the dream of his mother before she is pregnant. This is the beginning of the birth of the Buddha. The Queen Siri Maha Maya's dream that the Bodhisava was invited to descend from the Dusit heaven [1-3].

Figure 7.3: The mother's dream

The Picture 2: The birth

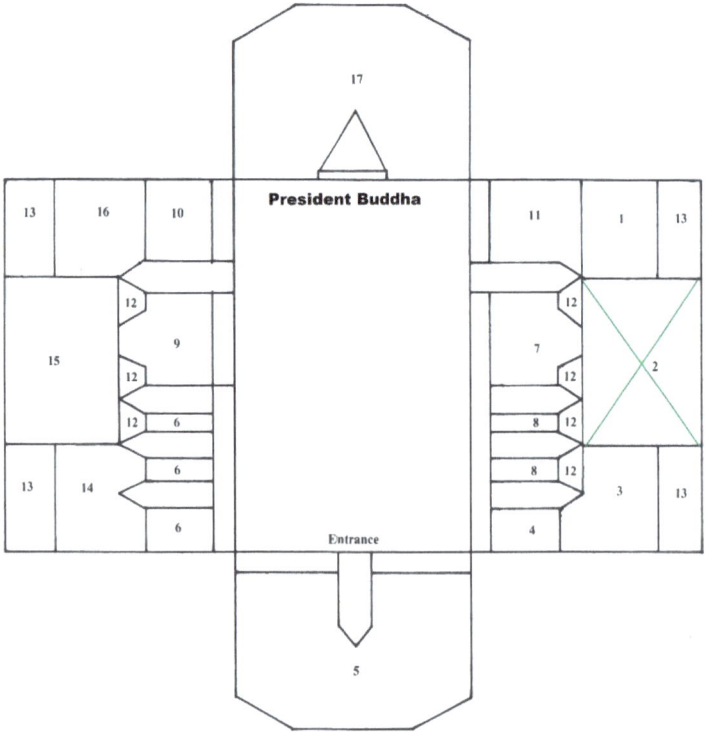

Figure 7.4: The Ubosatha hall layout of the birth picture

Figure 7.5: The birth pictures (green circle picture)

This picture is about the birth of the Buddha. When the Queen Siri Maha Maya arrived at the Lumphini park, which it is half way between the city of Kapilavastu and Thewathaha.

Figure 7.6: The birth pictures

The Queen was standing while labour and give birth. The child walks seven steps on the lotus after birth. This is not realistic, but the imagination to create a miracle. [1-3]

The Picture 3: The five revelations dream

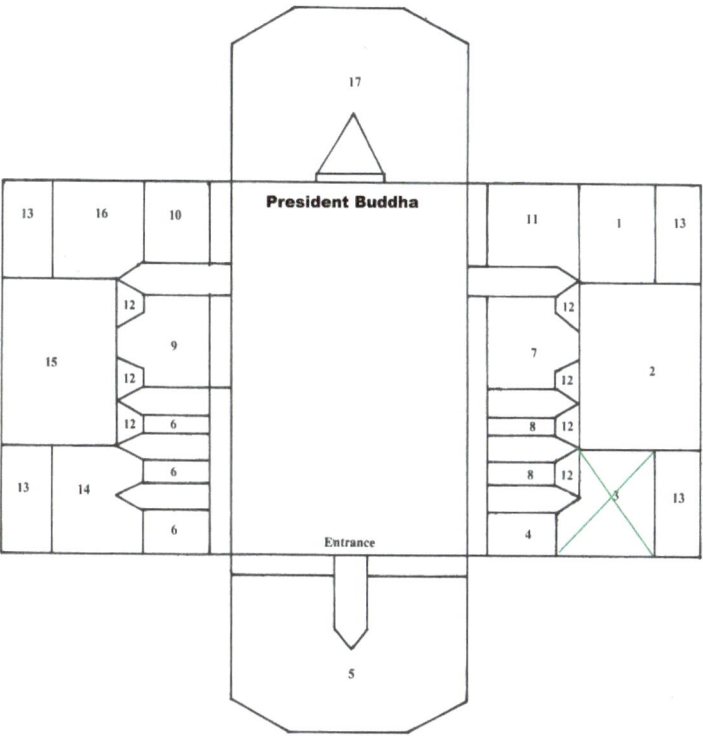

Figure 7.7: The Ubosatha hall layout of the five revelations dream picture

Figure 7.8: The dream of five revelations (green circle picture)

This picture is about the dream of the five revelations.

After the Buddha self mortification and not obtain the enlightenment. Thus, he begins eating and has a dream that he lay on the ground, his head on the Himavanta mountain, his left hand on in the east sea and his right hand in the south sea.

A lot of worms crawl on his left foot and knee. A grass grows from his navel. All colourful birds change to white colour when landing on him. When he practises walking meditation in the mountain with full of excrement, but his feet are clean. [1-3]

Figure 7.9: The dream of five

The meaning of his dreams is the five revelations, which includes he would reach the enlightenment. He would have a lot of followers. He would teach the Dhamma to all humanity. Everybody and every society would benefit from the Dhamma. His mind would remain purify. [1-3]

The Picture 4: The casting the tray fortune

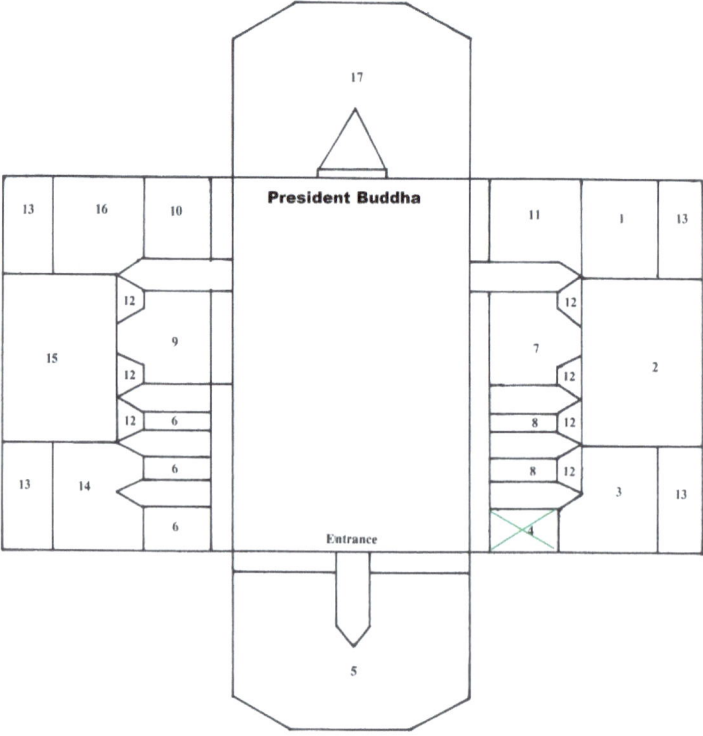

Figure 7.10: The Ubosatha hall layout of the casting the tray fortune picture

Figure 7.11: The casting the tray fortune (green circle picture)

This picture is about the casting tray to predict the future. The Buddha places the tray on the water and ask for a predict that if his merits had been sufficient to attain the Buddha, the tray may float upstream.

Figure 7.12: The casting the tray

CHAPTER 8

Pictures Plan 5-7

The Picture 5: The fight with the King of Mara

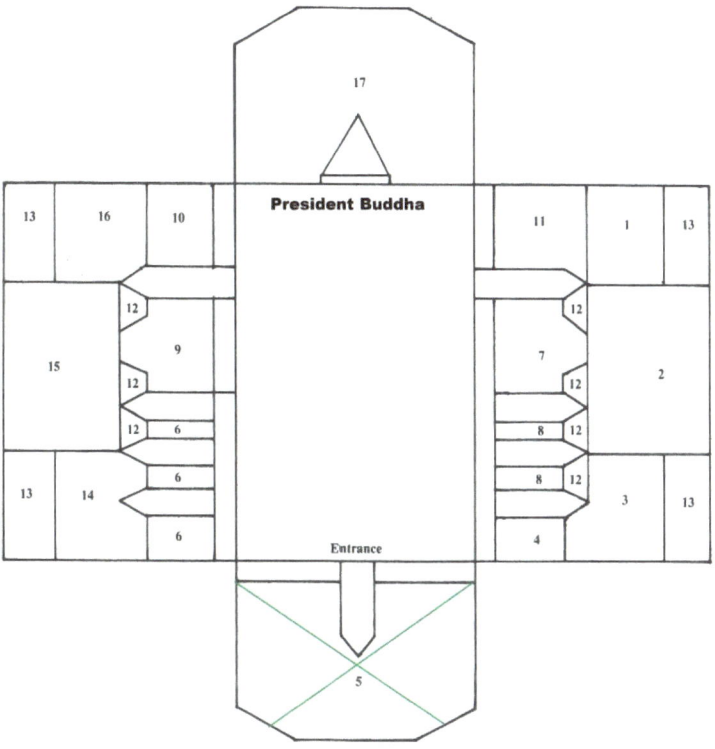

Figure 8.1: The Ubosatha hall layout of the fight with the King of Mara picture

Figure 8.2: The fight with the King of Mara (green circle picture)

This picture is about the enlightenment and defeat the King of Mara and the evil army.

Figure 8.3: The Buddha defeats the King of Mara

The King of Mara is the evil, learn that the Buddha would bring an end to his kingdom. Therefore, he decides to attack the Buddha with his army. However, all of his weapons were useless and become flowers and garlands.

Figure 8.4: The Earth Goddess (green circle picture)

In addition, he challenges the Buddha that the magnificent throne does not belong to him. The Earth Goddess is the witness that the Buddha has accumulated merits for a long time. To prove how long it is, thus she squeezes her long hair and water flood over the whole army.

The Picture 6: The four levels of lotus

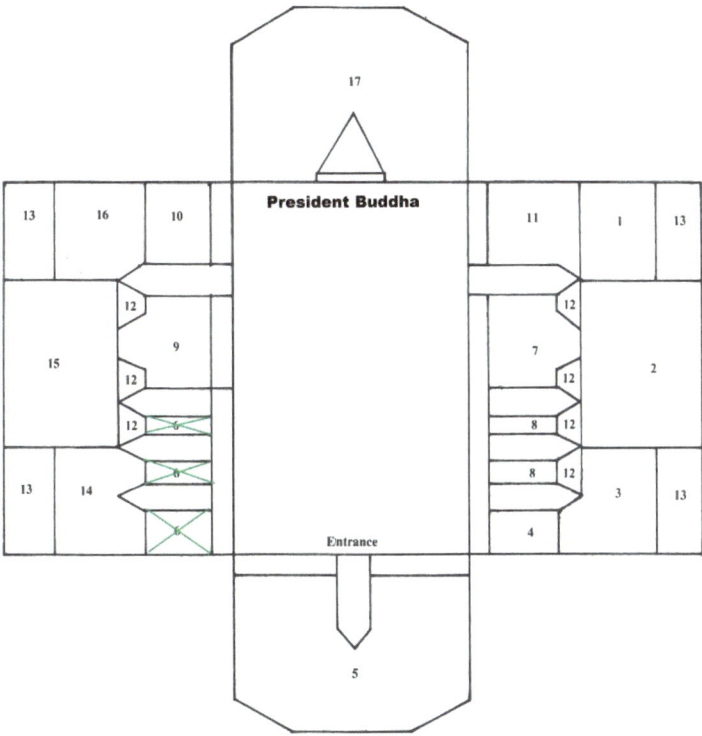

Figure 8.5: The Ubosatha hall layout of the four levels of lotus picture

Figure 8.6: The four levels of lotus on the right wall corner (green circle picture)

This picture is about the four groups of the lotus, which compare to four levels of humans. The first group is the lotus in the air. This lotus is in the perfect condition, which ready to bloom and just waiting for the Sun shine to grow big and become the beautiful lotus. This compares to people, who is ready and can understand Dthamma easily.

The second group is the lotus in the lotus just above the water. This group of lotus just needs more time to grow. This group compares to the people, who just needs a little bit of advice or learning in order to achieve successful.

Figure 8.7: The four levels of lotus

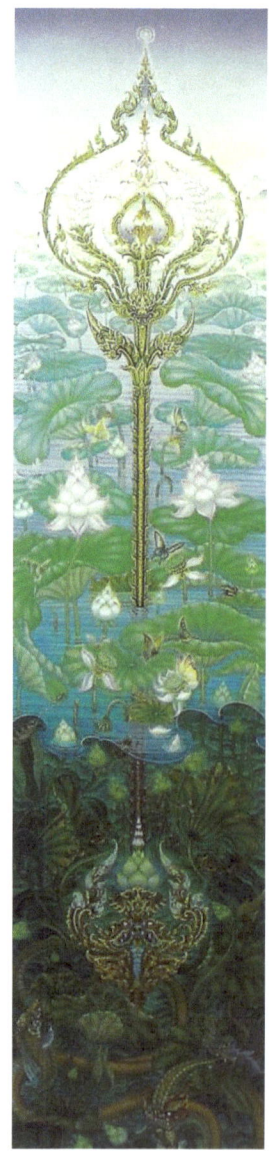

Figure 8.8: The four levels of lotus

Figure 8.9: The four levels of lotus

Figure 8.10: The four levels of lotus

Figure 8.11: The four levels of lotus on the right wall centre (green circle picture)

The third group is the lotus under the water. This lotus has a 50% chance to survive and a 50% chance to be eaten by the fisheries. This group compares to people, who could or could not be taught to under the Dhamma.

The final group is the lotus under the ground. This lotus would become the food for the fishes and animals. This group compares to the people, who have no ability to understand the Dhamma at all.

The Picture 7: The first sermon

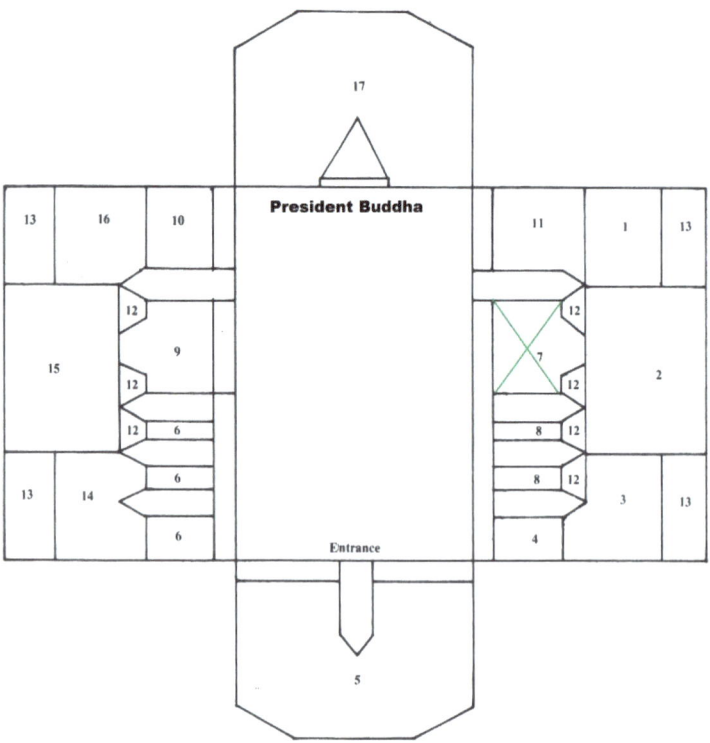

Figure 8.12: The Ubosatha hall layout of the first sermon picture

Figure 8.13: The first sermon (green circle picture)

This picture is about the Buddha's first sermon. After the Buddha reaches the enlightenment, he would like to give his first sermon to the five followers, who used to look after him when he had practiced torment self-mortification.

The Buddha tells them that he reached the enlightenment and this would help them to understand the truth of the human life cycle.

Therefore, on the full moon day of the eighth lunar month, the Buddha delivered his first sermon, which is called the Dhammajakra Krappawana Sutra.

Figure 8.14: The first sermon

CHAPTER 9
Pictures Plan 8-10

The Picture 8: The Thammajakra Kappawatana Sutra

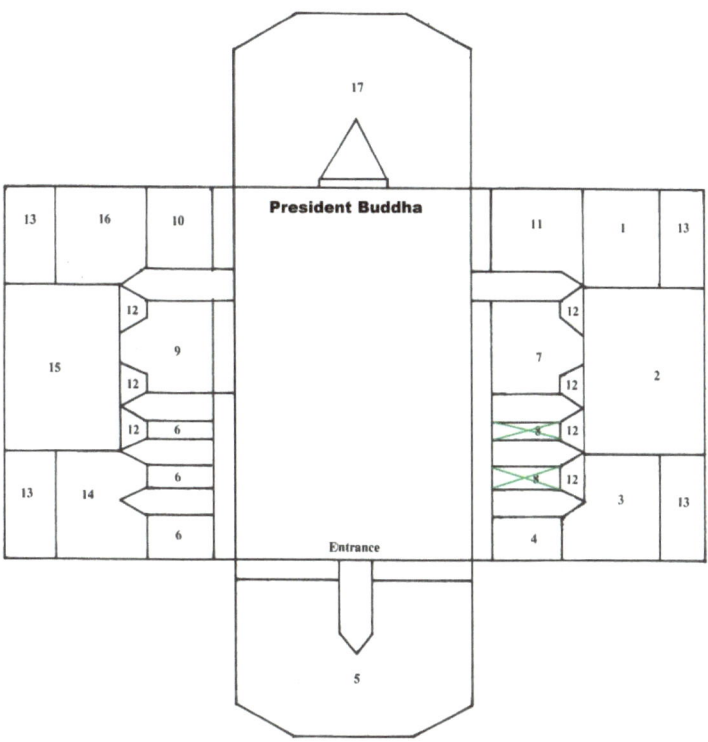

Figure 9.1: The Ubosatha hall layout of the Thammajakra Kappawatana Sutra picture

Figure 9.2: The Thammajakra Kappawatana Sutra (green circle picture)

This picture is about the first Dhamma, which call Thammajakra Kappawatana Sutr, that the Buddha gives to the five followers.

There are two main concepts for the monks in order to reach the enlightenment and nirvana, they are in the Dhammajakra Krappawana Sutra.

The first concept is the extreme self mortification. The second concept is the loose discipline. Both of these ways are not the right way to reach the enlightenment.

Figure 9.3: The loose discipline

Figure 9.4: The extreme self mortification

However, the right way is the middle practice between the loose discipline and the extreme self mortification is the best way.

There are eight ways to practice, it's called the Noble Eightfold Path, which includes right view, right thought, right speech, right action, right livelihood, right effort, right mindfulness and right concentration.

The Picture 9: The Buddha teaches the Dhamma to his mother and go to teach in the Hell World

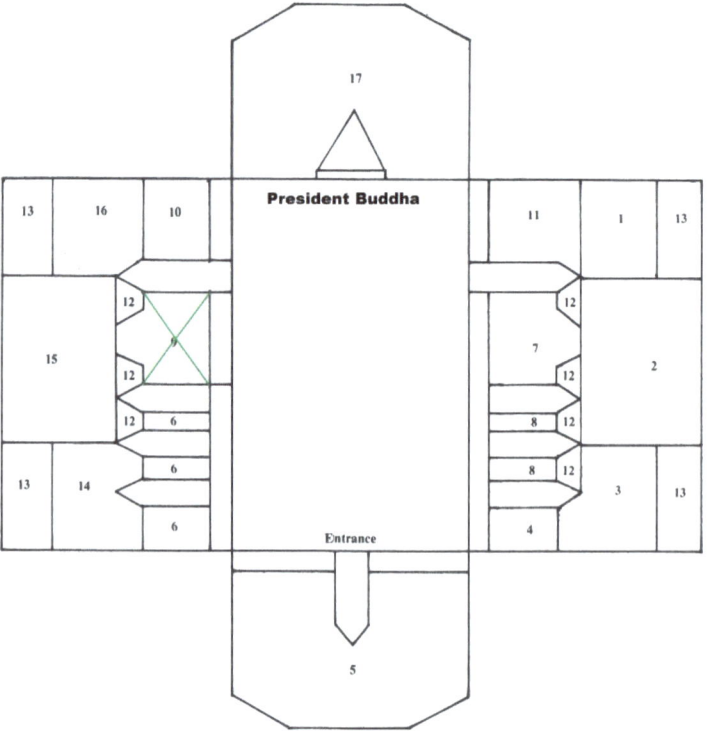

Figure 9.5: The Ubosatha hall layout of the Buddha teaches the Dhamma to his mother and go to teach in the Hell World picture

This picture is about travel to the heaven and teach the Dhamma to his mother.

Figure 9.6: Teach Dhamma to mother (green circle picture)

Figure 9.7: The Buddha teaches Dhamma to his mother

After the Buddha performs the first and the second miracle, he goes to the heaven at the Tavatimsa level to visit his mother and teach her the Dhamma.

He stays there for 3 months before descending and perform ten directions miracle reveal the Heaven World, the Human World and the Hell World.

Figure 9.8: The Buddha descent from the heaven to teach the Dhamma to the Hell World

The Picture 10: The two miracles

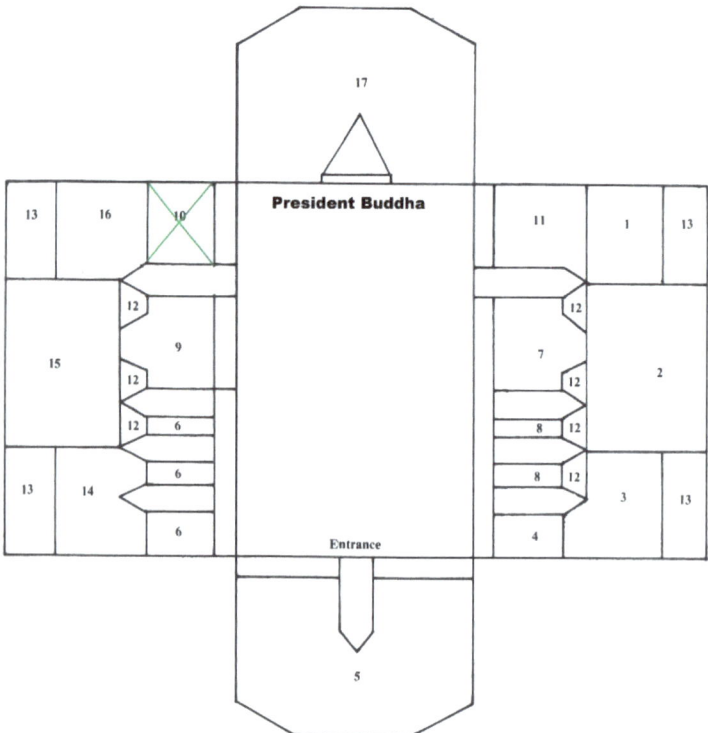

Figure 9.9: The Ubosatha hall layout of the two miracles picture

Figure 9.10: The two miracles (green circle picture)

This picture is about present two miracles that the Buddha performs.

Figure 9.11: The first miracle

The Buddha performs the first miracle when there is a flooding in the city and he practices walking meditation on the water. There are a lot of people on the boat comes to see and witness this miracle.

Figure 9.12: The Buddha's students perform fly action to get the bowl down

Figure 9.13: The second miracle

The Buddha performs the second miracle under the mango tree in many postures such as sit, walking, standing and reclining.

The cause of the challenge from the rich merchant about there is not worthy of reverence if there is no monks cannot fly to get the alms bowl from the top of the tree.

Thus, one of the Buddha's students perform fly action to get the bowl down. However, the Buddha does not want people to believe the Dhamma and respect the monks because of the superhuman performance.

The second miracle is special because the Buddha announce in advance that he will perform the miracle under the mango tree. The people who do not like him cut all of the mango trees in the city. Their purpose to make sure that there is no mango trees left of the Buddha to perform the miracle.

When the Buddha arrives at the park, there are no mango trees left. However, the park keeper offers him the ripe mango. After the Buddha eats that mango, he asks the park keeper to plant the seed and the Buddha wash his hands over the mango seed. The mango tree from that seed grows instantly in front many people.

CHAPTER 10

Pictures Plan 11

The Picture 11: The eight miracles

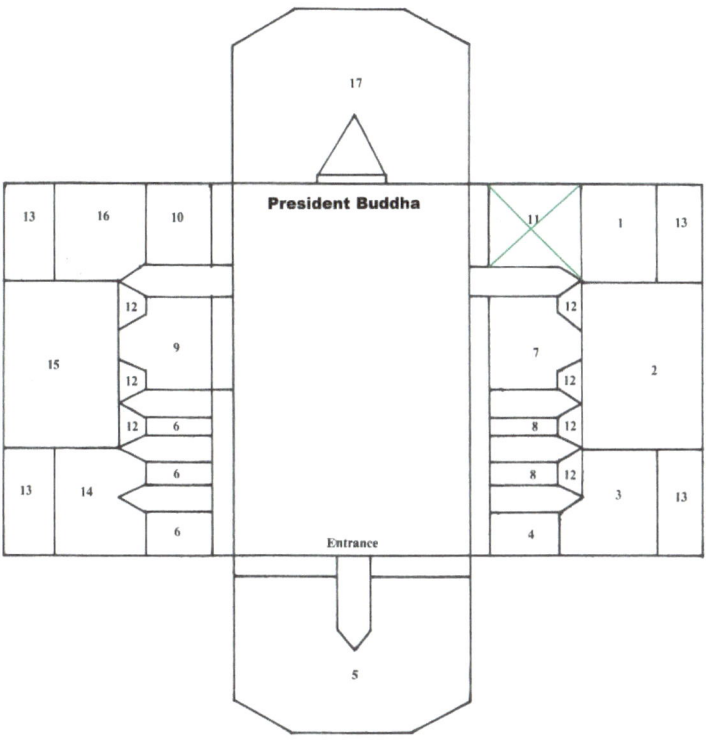

Figure 10.1: The Ubosatha hall layout of the eight miracles picture

Figure 10.2: The eight miracles (green circle picture)

This picture is about present eight miracles. The Buddha performs eight miracles. The first miracle is to perform defeating the King of Mara, name Wasawadi. The second miracle is defeating the giant, name Alawaka.

The third miracle is to perform defeating the elephant, name Nakakiri. The fourth miracle is to perform defeating the thief, name Angkhuliman. The fifth miracle is to perform defeating the woman, name Jinjamanavika.

The sixth miracle is to perform defeating the heretic, name Satjakanikkaron. The seventh miracle is to perform defeating the Naga, name Nantopananta. The eighth miracle is to perform defeating the Pakabrahma.

Figure 10.3: The second miracles defeating the King of Mara Wasawadi

Figure 10.4: The second miracles defeating the giant Alawaka

Figure 10.5: The third miracles defeating the elephant Nakakiri

Figure 10.6: The fourth miracles defeating the thief Angkhuliman

Figure 10.7: The fifth miracles defeating the woman Jinjamanavika

Figure 10.8: The sixth miracles defeating the heretic Satjakanikkaron

Figure 10.9: The seventh miracles defeating the Naga Nantopananta

Figure 10.10: The eighth miracles defeating the Thao Pakabrahma

CHAPTER 11

Pictures Plan 12

The Picture 12: The seven days Buddha

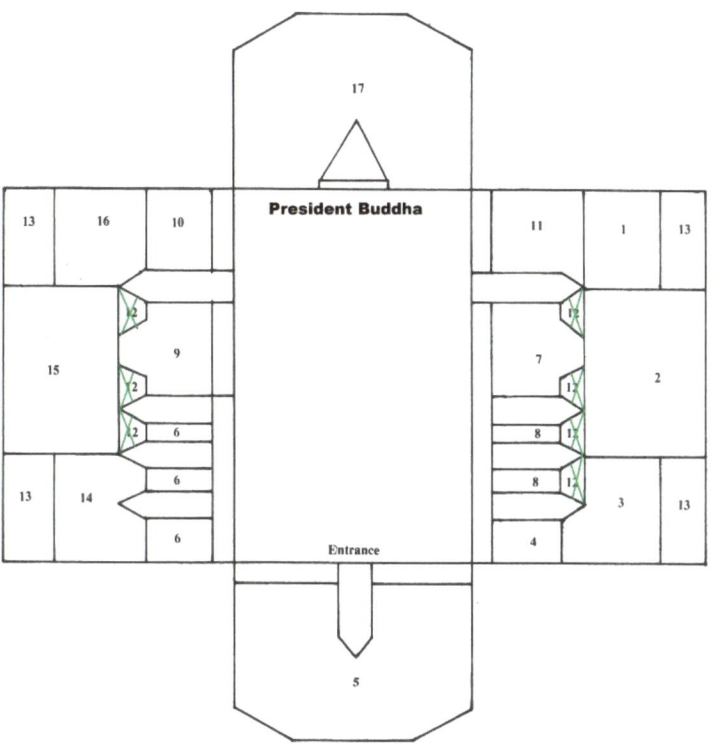

Figure 11.1: The Ubosatha hall layout of the Buddha action for every day in a week picture

Figure 11.2: The Sunday to Wednesday Buddha (green circle picture)

The seven days Buddha. This is a Buddha action for every day in a week.

On the left hand wall of the presiding Buddha in the Ubosatha hall, is the Buddha for the Sunday, Monday, Tuesday, and Wednesday.

On the right hand wall of the presiding Buddha in the Ubosatha hall is the Buddha for the Thursday, Friday and Saturday.

Figure 11.3: The Thursday to Saturday Buddha (green circle picture)

In Buddha calender, the first day of the week is Sunday. The Monday is the second day of the week and the Saturday is the last day of the week.

Therefore, on the right hand size of the president Buddha of the Ubosatha hall at the Buddhapadipa temple, the first Buddha day is Sunday.

The Sunday Buddha story about the Buddha reaches the enlightenment after sitting meditation under the big tree for seven days. Then, he stands up and look at the big tree for seven days without closing his eyes. This is to pay respect to the tree.

Figure 11.4: The Sunday Buddha

The Buddha action on the Sunday is standing. His eyes open and look toward the front, but not far, just couple meters from his feet. His hands are positioned in front of his body in front of his stomach. The right hand is placed over the left hand.

Figure 11.5: The Monday Buddha

The Buddha action on the Monday is standing. His right hand is raised in the chest position, while the left hand lay along his body. This act is from when the Buddha helps people from the epidemic in the city.

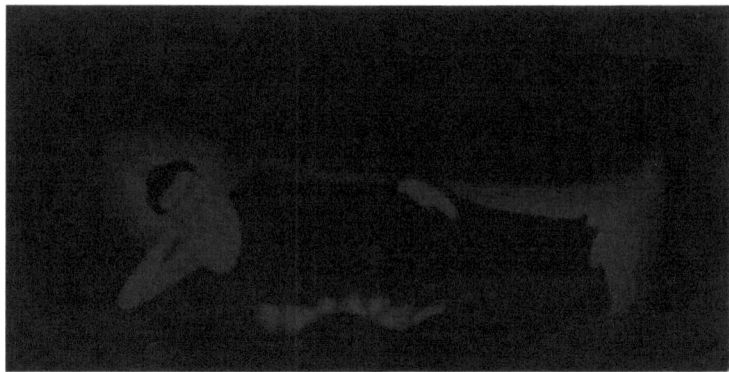

Figure 11.6: The Tuesday Buddha

The Buddha action on the Tuesday lays down side way position. He lay on his right side. Both feet together, the left foot on top of the right foot. His left hand leaning on his body and his right hand in the position to support his head as a pillow.

The story about this Tuesday Buddha is when the demon understands that he has the biggest body that everybody. Therefore, the Buddha creates his body bigger than the demon, in order to teach him that his understanding is wrong.

Figure 11.7: The Wednesday Buddha

The Buddha action on the Wednesday is standing and both hands are in front of his body and carry the alms bowl. The story about this Wednesday Buddha is the Buddha goes out in the morning to receive alms from people in the city since his royal relatives forgot to invite him for the morning food.

Figure 11.8: The Thursday Buddha

The Buddha action on the Thursday is sitting, meditation and reach the enlightenment. Both of his hands are on his lap position. His right hand is placed over his left hand. He sits cross legs, his right leg on top of his left leg.

The story about this Thursday Buddha is after the Buddha defeats the King of Mara. He concentrates in practise his meditation until he reaches the enlightenment on the Visakha Bucha day.

Figure 11.9: The Friday Buddha

The Buddha action on the Thursday is standing. Both of his hands are on the chest level. His right hand is placed on top of his left hand.

The story about this Friday Buddha is after the Buddha reaches the enlightenment and he realises that his Dhamma is very difficult to understand. However, he gives the Dhamma to suit the different levels.

Figure 11.10: The Saturday Buddha

The Buddha action on the Saturday is sitting cross legs. His right hand is placed on top over his left hand and his right leg is over his left leg. There is a big Nakha spread their heads over his head.

The story about this Friday Buddha is when the Buddha practises his meditation. There is non stop raining for seven days. The King of Na Kha spreads his seven heads to shelter the rain for the Buddha.

CHAPTER 12
Pictures Plan 13-14

The Picture 13: The celestial assembly

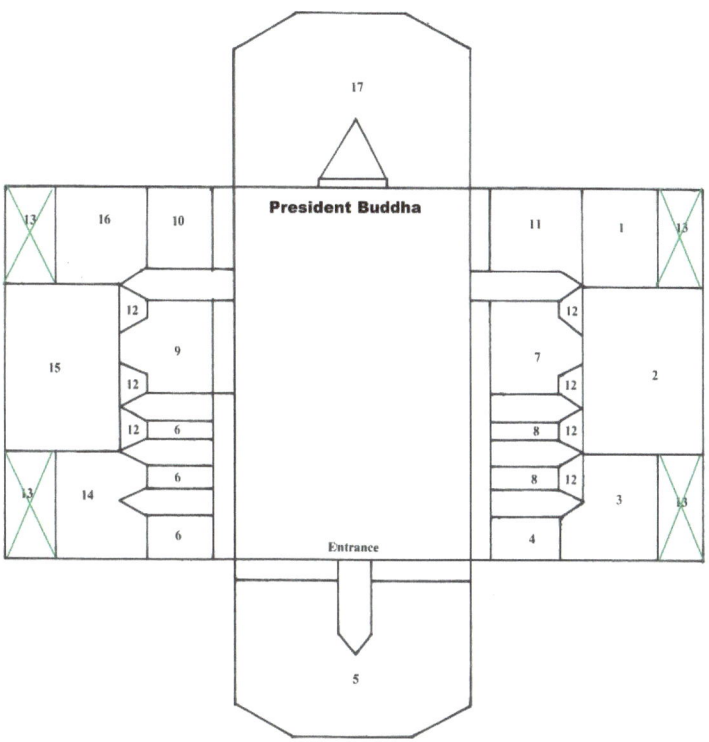

Figure 12.1: The Ubosatha hall layout of the celestial assembly picture

Figure 12.2: The celestial assembly on the far end of the left wall (green circle picture)

This picture is about the celestial assembly. There are four sets of these pictures. They are two pictures on the left wall and two pictures on the right wall.

Figure 12.3: The celestial assembly on the birth of the Buddha

Figure 12.4: The celestial assembly on the corner left wall (green circle picture)

Figure 12.5: The celestial assembly on the birth of the Buddha

Figure 12.6: The celestial assembly on the right corner (green circle picture)

Figure 12.7: The celestial assembly on the death of the Buddha

Figure 12.8: The celestial assembly on the far end of the right wall (green circle picture)

Figure 12.9: The celestial assembly on the death of the Buddha

A group of these celestial comes to pay the respect to the Buddha in the important events such as the birth of the Buddha and the death of the Buddha.

The Picture 14: the Mara King asks the Buddha to death and the Buddha's last meal

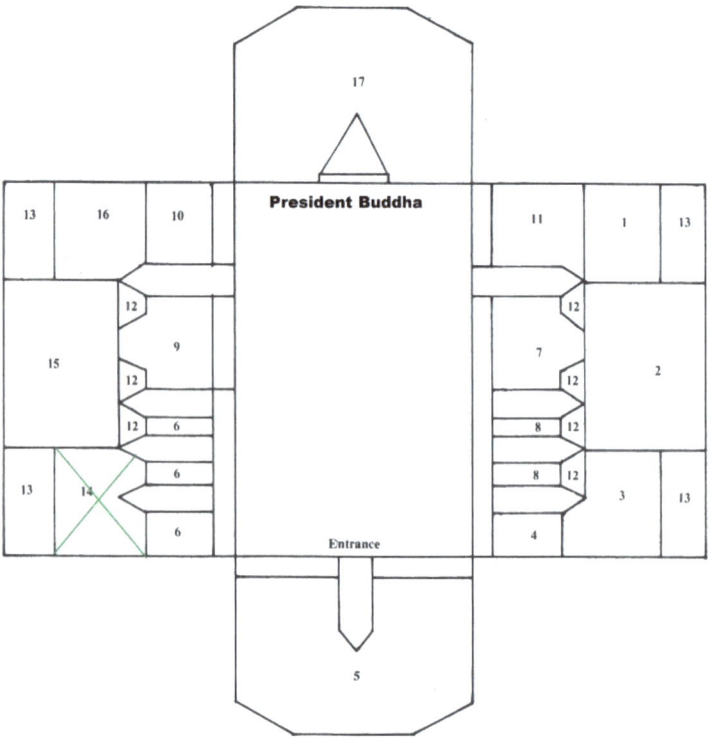

Figure 12.10: The Ubosatha hall layout of the Mara King asks the Buddha to death and the Buddha's last meal pictures

Figure 12.11: Mara King asks the Buddha to death or Nirvana (green circle picture)

Figure 12.12: The King of Mara and the Buddha

These pictures are about the Mara King asks the Buddha to death or nirvana and the Buddha's last meal before he become ill and later die.

When the King of Mara asks the Buddha to death, his answer is it is not the time for him to die yet. It will be another 3 more months. This story shows that the Buddha knows the date when he will pass away.

Figure 12.13: The last meal (green circle picture)

The last meal picture shows the Buddha has his meal with other monks. However, he asks the house owner do not give this dish that offer food him to other monks, but buries them in the ground. This shows he might know that the food may create the sickness.

Figure 12.14: The Buddha's last meal

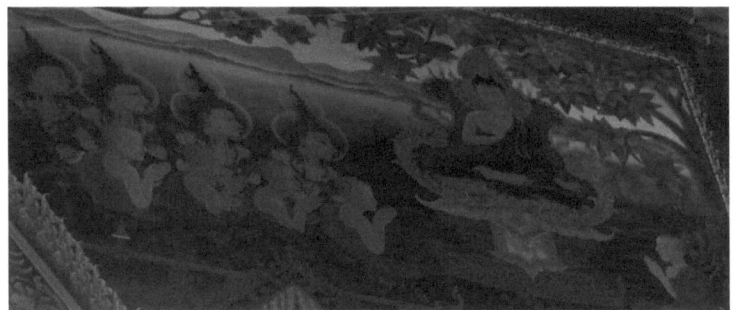

Figure 12.15: The Buddha becomes ill

CHAPTER 13
Pictures Plan 15-16

The Picture 15: The death of the Buddha

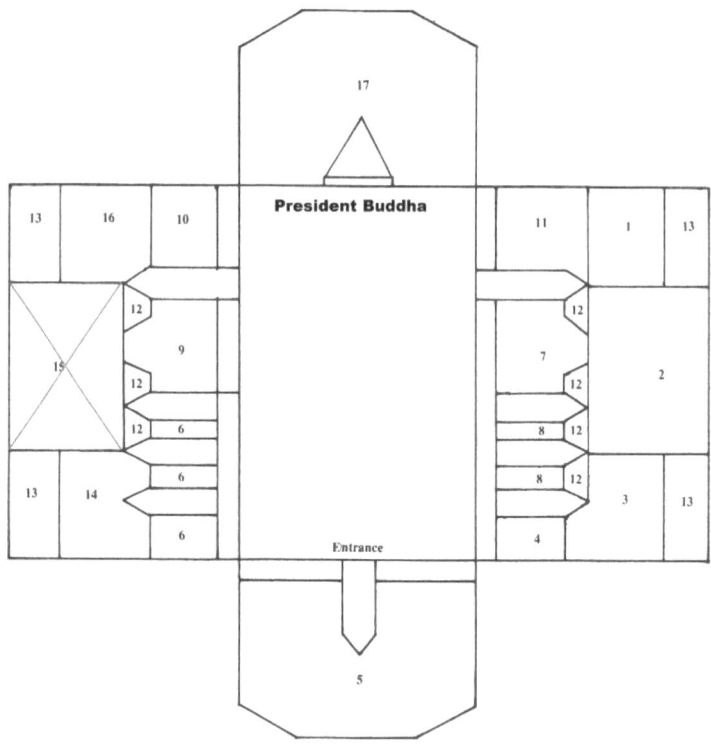

Figure 13.1: The Ubosatha hall layout of the death of the Buddha picture

Figure 13.2: The death of the Buddha or the Nirvana (green circle picture)

This picture is about the death of the Buddha or the Buddha's Nirvana.

Figure 13.3: The death of the Buddha

This picture is the biggest in this right wall. It shows the most important story. There are not only the monks, but also the celestial and animals come to pay last respect to the Buddha before he passes away.

The tree on the left and right curve to each other to show the sorrow. A golden palace floating above the Buddha, it means the pure mind of the Buddha.

The man in white dress is the Brahmin, Suphataparipachok, he is the last disciple of the Buddha.

The flowers, it's name the flower Montha, lay on the ground when the Buddha passes away.

The Picture 16: The Buddha's relics

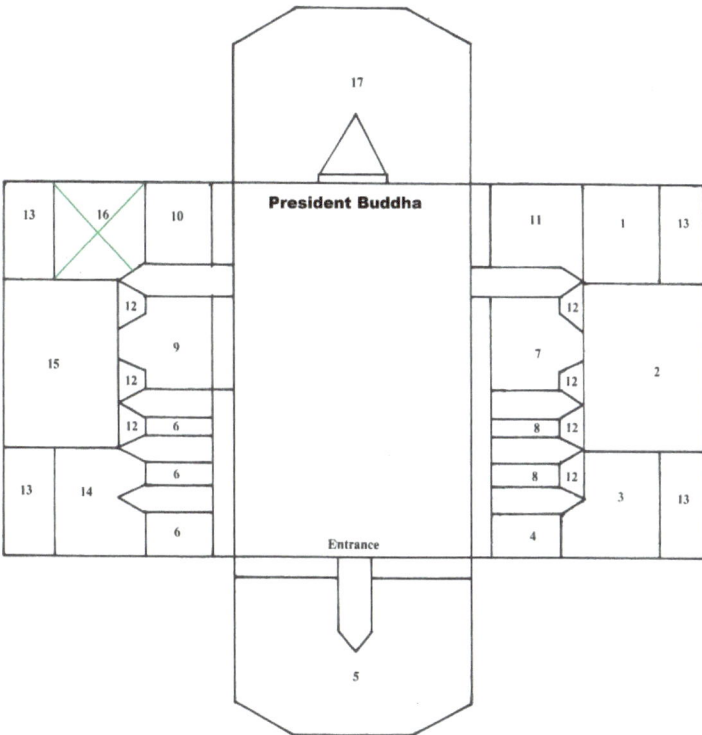

Figure 13.4: The Ubosatha hall layout of the flower Montha and the Buddha's relics picture

Figure 13.5: The divided the Buddha's relics (green circle picture)

This picture is about the Buddha's cremation and divided his relics.

The Montha flowers lay on the ground when the Buddha passes away. When the hunters carry the flower Montra in their hands, this flower is the signal to tell the Buddha's students know that the Buddha passes away.

Figure 13.6: The Montha flower

Figure 13.7: The divided the Buddha's relics

The man in white dress, the Brahim Tona, divided the Buddha's relics to many Kingdoms, both in the heaven and human world.

CHAPTER 14
Pictures Plan 17

The Picture 17: The three worlds

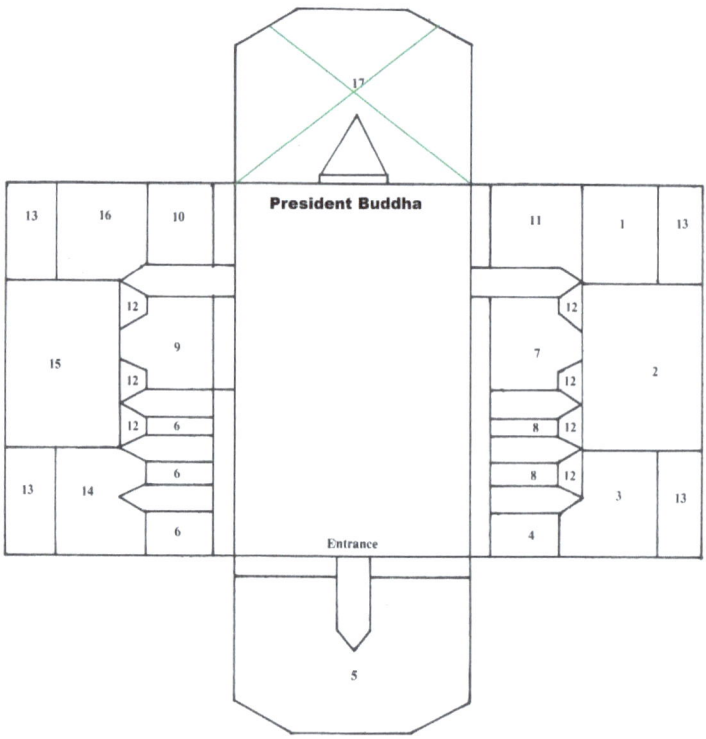

Figure 14.1: The Ubosatha hall layout of the three world pictures

Figure 14.2: The three worlds (green circle picture)

This picture is about the three words: the Heaven world, the Human world and the Hell world.

14.1 The Hell world

The lowest part of the picture in this the black dark wall, which represent the hell world. Normally, it would mean the world beneath the earth or underground. This world is lower than the human world.

Figure 14.3: The Hell world

Figure 14.4: The Hell World (green circle picture)

The characteristic of the hell world is dark and extremely hot from the heat from the fire. All animals and people live there are suffering, sad and unhappy.

Figure 14.5: The Buddha in the Hell World

However, this is an imaginary world, not realistic. There may reference from the science and geography of the earth that at the core of the earth, the temperature is higher than the surface. In addition, the sunshine would not reach the inner part of the earth.

Therefore, it would be dark, no plants, no trees and nothing grow. Some animals live there needs to adjust and adapt in order to survive the environment. Thus, they need to mutate their shape and body.

14.2 The human world

Figure 14.6: The Human World (green circle picture)

The human world shows people in the cheerful mood, living style, temples and meditation. This world is important because the Buddha reaches enlightenment in this human world. Therefore, it has the most effect to people in this human world more than the hell and the heaven world.

People in this world would believe and practice the Dhamma and practice follows the Buddha method. Thus, the highest purpose of people in the human world is reaching at the enlightenment and get to the Nirvara.

Figure 14.7: The people in the Human World

Figure 14.8: The monks in the Human World

The pictures of human world would show the residential areas, houses and people with many activities involve with the merit and temple such as offer food to the monks.

Figure 14.9: The Buddha reaches the enlightenment in the Human World

In the centre of the human world, it shows the meaning of the enlightenment. The big pink lotus under the Buddha is the connection point between the human world and the heaven world. The vertical line in the centre means the high intention to follow the Dhamma to reach the Nirvana World.

The picture on this wall is the triangle shape, which means everything aims to reach the Nirvana. In addition, the triangle also means Sila, Samathi and Panya.

There are four lotus grow out of the big pink lotus, which means suffering, cause of the suffering, how to get rid of the suffering, and the eight path practise.

There are two lamps on each side of the golden triangle, locate above the edge of the human world represent the light of the Dhamma, which are above the four wooden houses in the human world.

Figure 14.10: The Heaven World (green circle picture)

14.3 The Heaven World

The Heaven World as the artist's imaginary, there are many palaces in the heaven. The heaven boundary starts from the six palaces at the same level as the big pink lotus. They are on the green sea level, which show some fish eats each other fish. This means that the heaven still has some desires.

The lowest level of the celestial, their palace just above the human world and they still have their desire.

Figure 14.11: The six Heaven above the Sithandara Ocean

Figure 14.12: The three heavens on the right and three on the left

In addition, there are many level classes of celestial higher than the heaven. There are sixteen level palaces of the Phrum and Prahma. This includes the five levels of the Suthavas, which are higher than the six heavens.

Figure 14.13: The sixteen Brahma levels

The higher level of Brahma, the highest of their mind. The clear flower means how clearly mind of the Brahma at the high level.

Figure 14.14: The four non- form Prahma

Another two pictures each side in light pink and circle are present the non-form of the Prahma, totally four palaces. The clear flowers float around the palaces mean the enjoy, happy and clear mind of the Prahma.

Figure 14.15: The list of Buddha

There are five Buddhas, they are Kakusantho, Konakom, Kasapa, Kodom and Ariyametai. The middle one is the present Buddha Kodom, who is the present. The next one Buddha would be the Ariyametai.

REFERENCES

1 C. Kositpipat, P. Vijinthanasarn and S. Budrat, "The Mural Paintings of Wat Buddhapadipa".

2 C. Kositpipat and P. Vijinthanasarn, "The Mural Paintings of Wat Buddhapadipa".

3 C. Kositpipat, P. Vijinthanasarn and S. Budrat, "The Mural Paintings of Wat Buddhapadipa", 2018.

www.ingramcontent.com/pod-product-compliance
Lightning Source LLC
Chambersburg PA
CBHW041621220426
43662CB00001B/2